THE KIDNEY TRANSPLANT DIET COOKBOOK

Susan Stowers

TABLE OF CONTENT

Introduction

● Understanding Your Post-Transplant Diet

A kidney transplant is a life-changing event, opening doors to renewed health and a brighter future.

However, it also marks the beginning of a new relationship with your body, one that requires special attention to nutrition.

Understanding your post-transplant diet is crucial for supporting your recovery, maintaining the health of your new kidney, and minimizing potential complications.

This book, **"The Kidney Transplant Diet Cookbook,"** is dedicated to helping you grasp the intricacies of your post-transplant nutritional needs.

It's not just about restrictions; it's about making informed food choices that promote healing and enhance your overall well-being.

Here's what you need to know about your post-transplant diet:

1. Why is it different?

Your new kidney, along with the anti-rejection medications you'll be taking, influence your dietary requirements.

These medications can affect your body's ability to process certain nutrients, making it essential to monitor your intake of sodium, potassium, phosphorus, and fluids.

2. What are the key goals?

Protect your new kidney: A balanced diet helps prevent stress on your kidney and reduces the risk of rejection.

Manage medication side effects: Proper nutrition can help alleviate side effects like high blood pressure, fluid retention, and changes in blood sugar levels.

Support your immune system: A healthy diet strengthens your immune system, reducing the risk of infections.

Promote overall health: Good nutrition contributes to long-term health by reducing the risk of heart disease, diabetes, and other complications.

3. What are the key principles?

Control sodium intake: Excess sodium can lead to fluid retention and high blood pressure.

Monitor potassium levels: High potassium levels can cause heart problems.

Limit phosphorus: Elevated phosphorus levels can weaken bones.

Stay hydrated: Adequate fluid intake is essential for kidney function.

Prioritize nutrient-rich foods: Focus on fruits, vegetables, whole grains, lean proteins, and low-fat dairy.

4. How can this book help?

"The Kidney Transplant Diet Cookbook" provides:

Clear explanations: We break down complex dietary guidelines into easy-to-understand language.

Delicious recipes: We offer a variety of flavorful meals that are specifically designed to meet your post-transplant needs.

Practical tips: We provide guidance on meal planning, grocery shopping, and dining out.

This book is your partner in navigating your post-transplant journey.

By understanding your dietary needs and making informed choices, you can embrace a healthier, more vibrant future.

• Key Nutrients and Dietary Restrictions

Your kidney transplant marks a fresh start, a chance to reclaim your health and vitality. To support this new beginning, it's essential to understand the crucial connection between your diet and your well-being.

This chapter of "**The Kidney Transplant Diet Cookbook**" will illuminate the key nutrients your body needs and explain why certain dietary adjustments are necessary to protect your precious new organ.

Think of your diet as a foundation for your recovery and long-term health.

Just as a house requires strong building blocks, your body relies on essential nutrients to function optimally.

We'll explore these vital components, including:

Protein Powerhouses: Protein is crucial for cell growth and repair, especially after surgery.

We'll discuss how much protein you need and highlight excellent sources like lean meats, poultry, fish, eggs, and beans.

Carbohydrate Considerations: Carbohydrates provide energy, but it's important to choose the right kinds.

We'll focus on complex carbohydrates found in whole grains, fruits, and vegetables, which offer sustained energy and fiber.

Healthy Fats: Unsaturated fats, like those found in olive oil, avocados, and nuts, promote heart health. We'll explain why these fats are beneficial and how to incorporate them into your diet.

While nourishing your body is vital, it's equally important to be mindful of certain dietary restrictions.

These restrictions help protect your new kidney and prevent complications. We'll discuss:

Sodium Savvy: Too much sodium can raise blood pressure and strain your kidneys.

We'll provide practical tips for reducing sodium intake and identifying hidden sources in processed foods.

Potassium Control: Potassium plays a role in muscle and nerve function, but levels need to be carefully managed after a transplant.

We'll outline which foods are high in potassium and offer strategies for balancing your intake.

Phosphorus Prudence: High phosphorus levels can affect calcium absorption and bone health. We'll explain how to monitor phosphorus intake and make smart food choices.

Understanding these key nutrients and dietary restrictions empowers you to take charge of your health.

"The Kidney Transplant Diet Cookbook" will be your guide, providing delicious recipes and practical advice to make this journey both enjoyable and successful.

• Medications and Food Interactions

After a kidney transplant, your medications become vital allies in your recovery journey. These medications, primarily immunosuppressants, help prevent organ rejection and keep you healthy.

However, it's crucial to remember that these powerful drugs can interact with certain foods and nutrients, potentially affecting their efficacy and causing unwanted side effects.

Think of it like a delicate dance between your medications and your diet.

Each plays a critical role, but they need to be in sync to achieve the best possible outcome.

For example, grapefruit juice, while a healthy choice in many situations, can interfere with the metabolism of some immunosuppressants, leading to higher drug levels in your bloodstream. This could increase the risk of side effects.

On the other hand, some medications may hinder the absorption of essential nutrients like calcium or iron, emphasizing the need for a balanced diet and possibly even supplements.

Timing is also key. Taking certain medications with or without food can significantly impact their absorption and effectiveness.

For instance, some medications work best on an empty stomach, while others are better absorbed when taken with a meal.

Understanding these intricacies allows you to be proactive in your healthcare.

By being mindful of **potential food-medication** interactions, you can:

Maximize the effectiveness of your medications: Ensure your medications work as intended by avoiding foods that might interfere with their absorption or metabolism.

Minimize side effects: Reduce the risk of unwanted side effects by understanding which foods might exacerbate them.

Optimize nutrient absorption: Ensure you're getting the essential nutrients your body needs by adjusting your diet or considering supplements under the guidance of your healthcare provider.

Knowledge is power. By understanding the dynamic relationship between your medications and your diet, you can take control of your health, enhance your well-being, and savor the gift of a new beginning.

• Tips for Meal Planning and Grocery Shopping

Embarking on a kidney-transplant journey involves embracing a lifestyle that nurtures your overall well-being.

A significant part of this lifestyle shift involves adopting healthy eating habits.

Meal planning and grocery shopping, often considered mundane tasks, become powerful tools in your recovery arsenal.

They empower you to prioritize your nutritional needs, manage dietary restrictions, and savor the joy of food while supporting your health.

Think of meal planning as designing a personalized roadmap for your nutritional journey.

It's about making conscious choices that align with your dietary goals and restrictions.

Start by familiarizing yourself with the key principles of a kidney-friendly diet, such as limiting sodium, potassium, and phosphorus, while ensuring adequate protein intake.

Here are some strategies to streamline your meal planning process:

Create a Weekly Menu: Design a weekly menu that incorporates a variety of kidney-friendly foods.

This provides structure, reduces daily decision-making, and minimizes impulsive food choices.

Cook Once, Eat Twice: Prepare larger batches of food to enjoy as leftovers for another meal or freeze for future use.

This saves time and ensures you always have a nutritious meal on hand.

Embrace Variety: Include a rainbow of fruits and vegetables in your meals to ensure you receive a wide range of vitamins and minerals.

Prioritize Fresh Ingredients: Opt for fresh, whole foods whenever possible, such as lean meats, poultry, fish, fruits, vegetables, and whole grains.

Hydration is Key: Remember to drink plenty of fluids, primarily water, throughout the day to support your kidney function and overall health.

With a well-crafted meal plan in hand, grocery shopping becomes a purposeful mission.

Here's how to make your shopping trips efficient and effective:

Shop with a List: A detailed grocery list, organized by food categories, keeps you focused and prevents impulse purchases.

Read Labels Carefully: Pay close attention to nutrition labels, especially sodium, potassium, and phosphorus content.

Explore Fresh Produce: Visit the produce section first to stock up on fresh fruits and vegetables.

Choose Lean Protein Sources: Select lean cuts of meat, poultry without skin, and fish.

Embrace Whole Grains: Opt for whole-grain bread, pasta, rice, and cereals.

Limit Processed Foods: Minimize processed foods, which are often high in sodium, unhealthy fats, and additives.

By mastering the art of meal planning and grocery shopping, you transform these everyday tasks into opportunities to nourish your body, honor your new kidney, and embrace a healthier, more vibrant future.

Chapter 1: Breakfast Bites

1. Berry-Oatmeal Smoothie

Ingredients:

- 1 cup unsweetened almond milk (or other low-potassium milk alternative)
- 1/2 cup frozen mixed berries (like strawberries, blueberries, raspberries)
- 1/4 cup rolled oats
- 1 tablespoon almond butter
- 1/2 teaspoon chia seeds (optional)
- 1/4 teaspoon cinnamon

Instructions:

- Combine all ingredients in a blender.
- Blend until smooth and creamy.
- If too thick, add more almond milk. If too thin, add a few more frozen berries.

Serving Suggestion: Enjoy immediately.

2. Scrambled Eggs with Spinach and Mushrooms

Ingredients:

- 2 large eggs
- 1 tablespoon low-sodium milk or unsweetened almond milk
- 1/4 cup chopped spinach
- 1/4 cup sliced mushrooms
- 1 teaspoon olive oil
- Salt and pepper to taste (use sparingly)

Instructions:

- Heat olive oil in a nonstick skillet over medium heat.
- Add mushrooms and spinach; cook until softened.
- In a bowl, whisk together eggs and milk.
- Pour egg mixture into the skillet with the vegetables.
- Cook, stirring occasionally, until eggs are set.

- Season with salt and pepper (use sparingly).

Serving Suggestion: Serve with a slice of whole-wheat toast.

3. Apple Cinnamon Pancakes

Ingredients:

- 1 cup whole wheat flour
- 1 teaspoon baking powder
- 1/2 teaspoon baking soda
- 1/4 teaspoon salt
- 1 tablespoon sugar
- 1 teaspoon cinnamon
- 1 egg
- 1 cup low-fat milk (or milk alternative)
- 2 tablespoons unsalted butter, melted
- 1 small apple, peeled and diced

Instructions:

- In a large bowl, whisk together flour, baking powder, baking soda, salt, sugar, and cinnamon.

- In a separate bowl, whisk together egg, milk, and melted butter.
- Pour the wet ingredients into the dry ingredients and stir until just combined.
- Fold in the diced apple.
- Heat a lightly oiled griddle or frying pan over medium heat.
- Pour or scoop the batter onto the griddle, using approximately 1/4 cup for each pancake.
- Cook until bubbles form on the surface, then flip and cook until browned on the other side.

Serving Suggestion: Serve with a small amount of maple syrup or fresh fruit.

4. Whole Wheat Toast with Avocado and Tomato

Ingredients:

- 2 slices whole-wheat bread
- 1/2 avocado, mashed

- 1/4 tomato, sliced
- Salt and pepper to taste (use sparingly)

Instructions:

- Toast the bread.
- Spread mashed avocado on toast.
- Top with tomato slices.
- Season with salt and pepper (use sparingly).

Serving Suggestion: Enjoy as a quick and easy breakfast.

5. Yogurt Parfait with Granola and Fruit

Ingredients:

- 1 cup low-fat plain yogurt
- 1/4 cup low-sodium granola
- 1/2 cup mixed berries (or other low-potassium fruit)

Instructions:

- Layer yogurt, granola, and fruit in a glass or bowl.

Serving Suggestion: Enjoy immediately.

6. Breakfast Burrito with Turkey Sausage

Ingredients:

- 1 whole-wheat tortilla
- 2 ounces cooked turkey sausage, crumbled
- 1/4 cup scrambled eggs
- 1/4 cup chopped bell peppers and onions
- 1 tablespoon low-fat shredded cheese

Instructions:

- Warm the tortilla in a dry skillet or microwave.
- Fill the tortilla with turkey sausage, scrambled eggs, vegetables, and cheese.
- Fold the sides of the tortilla over the filling and roll up.

Serving Suggestion: Serve with salsa (check sodium content) or a small dollop of plain Greek yogurt.

7. Egg White Omelet with Veggies

Ingredients:

- 1/4 cup egg whites
- 1/4 cup chopped vegetables (onions, peppers, spinach, mushrooms)
- 1 teaspoon olive oil
- Salt and pepper to taste (use sparingly)

Instructions:

- Heat olive oil in a nonstick skillet over medium heat.
- Add vegetables and cook until softened.
- In a bowl, whisk egg whites until frothy.
- Pour egg whites into the skillet with the vegetables.
- Cook, lifting the edges to allow uncooked egg to flow underneath, until set.

- Season with salt and pepper (use sparingly).

Serving Suggestion: Serve with a side of fresh fruit.

8. Cream of Wheat with Berries

Ingredients:

- 1/2 cup quick-cooking cream of wheat
- 1 cup low-fat milk (or milk alternative)
- 1/4 cup mixed berries (or other low-potassium fruit)

Instructions:

- In a saucepan, bring milk to a simmer.
- Gradually whisk in cream of wheat.
- Cook, stirring constantly, until thickened.
- Top with berries.

Serving Suggestion: Enjoy warm.

9. French Toast with Fruit Salad

Ingredients:

- 2 slices whole-wheat bread
- 1 egg
- 1/4 cup low-fat milk (or milk alternative)
- 1/4 teaspoon cinnamon
- 1/2 cup mixed fruit (choose low-potassium options)

Instructions:

- In a shallow dish, whisk together egg, milk, and cinnamon.
- Dip bread slices in the egg mixture, coating both sides.
- Cook in a lightly oiled skillet or griddle over medium heat until golden brown on both sides.

Serving Suggestion: Serve with a side of fresh fruit salad.

10. Lox and Bagel with Low-Sodium Cream Cheese

Ingredients:

- 1 whole-wheat bagel, toasted
- 2 ounces smoked salmon (lox)
- 2 tablespoons low-sodium cream cheese

Instructions:

- Spread cream cheese on the toasted bagel.
- Top with smoked salmon.

Serving Suggestion: Enjoy with a side of sliced tomato and cucumber.

Important Notes for All Recipes:

Sodium: Use low-sodium or no-salt-added ingredients whenever possible. Be mindful of added salt and use it sparingly.

Potassium: Choose low-potassium fruits and vegetables. Some examples include berries, apples, grapes, green beans, and cauliflower.

Phosphorus: Limit dairy products and processed foods, which can be high in phosphorus.

Portion Control: Pay attention to portion sizes to manage calorie and nutrient intake.

Individual Needs: Always consult with your doctor or a registered dietitian for personalized dietary recommendations.

I hope these recipes provide a delicious and healthy start to your day!

Chapter 2: Lunchtime Favorites

11. Chicken Salad Lettuce Wraps

Ingredients:

- 2 cups cooked chicken breast, shredded or chopped (about 1 pound)
- ½ cup celery, finely chopped
- ½ cup red grapes, halved
- ¼ cup low-fat plain Greek yogurt
- 2 tablespoons mayonnaise (optional, use sparingly)
- 1 tablespoon Dijon mustard
- 1 tablespoon chopped fresh parsley
- Salt and pepper to taste (use sparingly)
- 8 large lettuce leaves, such as romaine or butter lettuce

Instructions:

- In a medium bowl, combine the chicken, celery, grapes, yogurt, mayonnaise (if using), mustard, and parsley.

- Season with salt and pepper to taste.
- Spoon the chicken salad mixture into the lettuce leaves.
- Serve immediately.

Cooking Time: No cooking required.

Serving Suggestions: Enjoy as a light and refreshing lunch or a healthy snack. For added flavor, top with a sprinkle of paprika or a squeeze of lemon juice.

12. Turkey and Avocado Sandwich on Whole Wheat Bread

Ingredients:

- 2 slices whole wheat bread
- 4 ounces sliced turkey breast
- ½ avocado, sliced
- 1 tablespoon low-fat mayonnaise (optional)
- 1 teaspoon Dijon mustard
- Lettuce and tomato slices, optional

Instructions:

- Spread mayonnaise (if using) and mustard on one slice of bread.
- Layer turkey, avocado, lettuce, and tomato (if using) on top.
- Top with the remaining slice of bread.
- Serve immediately.
- **Cooking Time**: No cooking required.

Serving Suggestions: This sandwich is a great source of protein and healthy fats. Pair it with a side salad or some fresh fruit for a complete meal.

13. Quinoa Salad with Roasted Vegetables

Ingredients:

- 1 cup quinoa, rinsed
- 2 cups vegetable broth (low sodium)
- 1 cup broccoli florets
- 1 cup Brussels sprouts, halved
- 1 cup carrots, chopped
- 2 tablespoons olive oil

- Salt and pepper to taste (use sparingly)
- 2 tablespoons lemon juice
- 2 tablespoons chopped fresh herbs (such as parsley, dill, or mint)

Instructions:

- Preheat oven to 400°F (200°C).
- Combine quinoa and vegetable broth in a saucepan. Bring to a boil, then reduce heat and simmer for 15-20 minutes, or until quinoa is cooked and liquid is absorbed.
- While quinoa is cooking, toss broccoli, Brussels sprouts, and carrots with olive oil, salt, and pepper on a baking sheet.
- Roast vegetables for 20-25 minutes, or until tender.
- In a large bowl, combine cooked quinoa, roasted vegetables, lemon juice, and fresh herbs.
- Serve warm or cold.
- **Cooking Time:** 40-45 minutes.

Serving Suggestions: This salad is a hearty and nutritious meal on its own. You can also add grilled chicken or fish for extra protein.

14. Lentil Soup with Whole Grain Bread

Ingredients:

- 1 cup brown or green lentils, rinsed
- 4 cups vegetable broth (low sodium)
- 1 onion, chopped
- 2 carrots, chopped
- 2 celery stalks, chopped
- 2 cloves garlic, minced
- 1 teaspoon dried thyme
- Salt and pepper to taste (use sparingly)
- 2 slices whole grain bread

Instructions:

- In a large pot, combine lentils, vegetable broth, onion, carrots, celery, garlic, and thyme.

- Bring to a boil, then reduce heat and simmer for 30-40 minutes, or until lentils are tender.
- Season with salt and pepper to taste.
- Serve with whole grain bread.
- Cooking Time: 40-50 minutes.

Serving Suggestions: This soup is a great source of protein and fiber. For a more substantial meal, serve with a side salad.

15. Tuna Salad with Crackers

Ingredients:

- 1 (5 ounce) can tuna, drained
- ¼ cup low-fat plain Greek yogurt
- 2 tablespoons mayonnaise (optional, use sparingly)
- 1 tablespoon Dijon mustard
- 1 tablespoon chopped celery
- Salt and pepper to taste (use sparingly)
- Whole grain crackers

Instructions:

- In a medium bowl, combine tuna, yogurt, mayonnaise (if using), mustard, and celery.
- Season with salt and pepper to taste.
- Serve with whole grain crackers.
- Cooking Time: No cooking required.

Serving Suggestions: This is a quick and easy lunch option. For a more complete meal, add a side salad or some fresh fruit.

16. Grilled Chicken Caesar Salad
(Dressing on the side)

Ingredients:

- 1 boneless, skinless chicken breast
- 1 tablespoon olive oil
- Salt and pepper to taste (use sparingly)
- 4 cups romaine lettuce, chopped
- ¼ cup grated Parmesan cheese
- Caesar salad dressing (low sodium, on the side)

Instructions:

- Preheat grill or grill pan to medium heat.
- Season chicken breast with olive oil, salt, and pepper.
- Grill chicken for 5-7 minutes per side, or until cooked through.
- Let chicken rest for a few minutes before slicing.
- In a large bowl, combine lettuce and Parmesan cheese.
- Top with sliced grilled chicken and serve with Caesar dressing on the side.
- **Cooking Time:** 15-20 minutes.

Serving Suggestions: This classic salad is a satisfying and healthy lunch option. Be mindful of the amount of dressing you use to control sodium intake.

17. Hummus and Veggie Wrap

Ingredients:

- 1 whole wheat tortilla
- ¼ cup hummus
- ½ cup mixed vegetables (such as carrots, cucumbers, bell peppers, and spinach)

Instructions:

- Spread hummus evenly over the tortilla.
- Top with mixed vegetables.
- Roll up the tortilla tightly.
- Serve immediately.
- **Cooking Time**: No cooking required.

Serving Suggestions: This wrap is a great source of protein and fiber. Pair it with a side of fruit or some whole grain crackers for a complete meal.

18. Leftover Roasted Chicken with a Side Salad

Ingredients:

- Leftover roasted chicken (skin removed)
- 4 cups mixed greens
- ½ cup cherry tomatoes, halved
- ¼ cup cucumber, sliced
- 2 tablespoons vinaigrette dressing (low sodium)

Instructions:

- In a large bowl, combine mixed greens, cherry tomatoes, and cucumber.
- Toss with vinaigrette dressing.
- Serve salad alongside leftover roasted chicken.
- **Cooking Time:** No cooking required.

Serving Suggestions: This is a quick and easy way to use up leftover chicken.

For a more substantial meal, add a side of quinoa or brown rice.

19. Black Bean Burger on a Whole Wheat Bun

Ingredients:

- 1 (15 ounce) can black beans, rinsed and drained
- ½ cup cooked brown rice
- ¼ cup chopped onion
- 2 cloves garlic, minced
- 1 tablespoon chili powder
- 1 teaspoon cumin
- Salt and pepper to taste (use sparingly)
- 1 whole wheat bun
- Lettuce, tomato, and onion, optional

Instructions:

- In a large bowl, mash black beans with a fork or potato masher.
- Add brown rice, onion, garlic, chili powder, cumin, salt, and pepper. Mix well.
- Form mixture into patties.

- Cook patties in a skillet over medium heat for 5-7 minutes per side, or until heated through.
- Serve on a whole wheat bun with desired toppings.
- **Cooking Time**: 15-20 minutes.

Serving Suggestions: This burger is a great source of protein and fiber. Pair it with a side salad or some baked sweet potato fries.

20. Pasta Salad with Grilled Chicken and Vegetables

Ingredients:

- 1 cup cooked pasta (whole wheat or gluten-free)
- 1 cup cooked chicken breast, cubed
- ½ cup cherry tomatoes, halved
- ½ cup cucumber, diced
- ¼ cup bell peppers, diced
- 2 tablespoons olive oil
- 2 tablespoons red wine vinegar

- 1 tablespoon Dijon mustard
- Salt and pepper to taste (use sparingly)

Instructions:

- In a large bowl, combine pasta, chicken, tomatoes, cucumber, and bell peppers.
- In a small bowl, whisk together olive oil, red wine vinegar, and mustard.
- Pour dressing over pasta salad and toss to coat.
- Season with salt and pepper to taste.
- Serve chilled.
- **Cooking Time:** 10-15 minutes.

Serving Suggestions: This salad is a hearty and flavorful lunch option. You can add other vegetables, such as broccoli or zucchini, for variety.

Important Notes for All Recipes:

Sodium: Use low-sodium or no-salt-added ingredients whenever possible. Be mindful of added salt and use it sparingly.

Potassium: If you need to limit potassium, be aware of high-potassium ingredients like bananas, potatoes, and tomatoes. Choose lower-potassium alternatives or limit portion sizes.

Phosphorus: If you need to limit phosphorus, be mindful of dairy products, beans, and nuts. Choose lower-phosphorus alternatives or limit portion sizes.

Freshness: Use fresh ingredients whenever possible for the best flavor and nutrition.

Customization: Feel free to adjust the ingredients and seasonings to your liking.

Remember to always consult with your doctor or registered dietitian for personalized dietary advice.

Chapter 3: Dinner Delights

21. Baked Salmon with Roasted Asparagus

Ingredients:

- 4 (4-ounce) salmon fillets, skin on or off
- 1 tablespoon olive oil
- 1 lemon, thinly sliced
- 1 pound asparagus, trimmed
- 1 teaspoon dried dill
- ½ teaspoon garlic powder
- Freshly ground black pepper to taste

Instructions:

- Preheat oven to 400°F (200°C). Line a baking sheet with parchment paper.
- Place salmon fillets on the prepared baking sheet. Drizzle with olive oil and top with lemon slices.

- In a bowl, toss asparagus with remaining olive oil, dill, garlic powder, and pepper. Arrange asparagus around the salmon.
- Bake for 12-15 minutes, or until salmon is cooked through and asparagus is tender-crisp.

Serving Suggestion: Serve with a side of brown rice or quinoa.

22. Lemon Herb Roasted Chicken with Brown Rice

Ingredients:

- 1 (3-4 pound) whole chicken
- 1 lemon, quartered
- 4 sprigs fresh rosemary
- 4 sprigs fresh thyme
- 1 tablespoon olive oil
- 1 teaspoon garlic powder
- ½ teaspoon dried oregano
- Salt and freshly ground black pepper to taste

- 1 cup brown rice, cooked according to package directions

Instructions:

- Preheat oven to 375°F (190°C).
- Rinse chicken and pat dry. Place lemon quarters and herbs inside the chicken cavity.
- Rub chicken with olive oil, garlic powder, oregano, salt, and pepper.
- Place chicken in a roasting pan and bake for 1 ½ - 2 hours, or until internal temperature reaches 165°F (74°C).
- Let chicken rest for 10 minutes before carving. Serve with brown rice.

Serving Suggestion: Add a side of steamed green beans or a mixed green salad.

23. Turkey Meatloaf with Mashed Sweet Potatoes

Ingredients:

- 1 ½ pounds ground turkey
- 1 cup breadcrumbs (whole wheat or gluten-free)
- ½ cup onion, finely chopped
- ½ cup bell pepper, finely chopped
- 1 egg, beaten
- ¼ cup ketchup (low-sodium)
- 1 tablespoon Worcestershire sauce (low-sodium)
- 1 teaspoon dried oregano
- ½ teaspoon garlic powder
- Salt and freshly ground black pepper to taste
- 2 large sweet potatoes, peeled and cubed

Instructions:

- Preheat oven to 350°F (175°C).

- In a large bowl, combine ground turkey, breadcrumbs, onion, bell pepper, egg, ketchup, Worcestershire sauce, oregano, garlic powder, salt, and pepper. Mix well.
- Shape mixture into a loaf and place in a baking dish.
- Bake for 1 hour, or until cooked through.
- While meatloaf is baking, boil sweet potatoes until tender. Drain and mash with a small amount of butter or olive oil (optional). Season with salt and pepper to taste.

Serving Suggestion: Serve meatloaf with mashed sweet potatoes and a side of steamed broccoli.

24. Shrimp Scampi with Zucchini Noodles

Ingredients:

- 1 pound large shrimp, peeled and deveined
- 2 tablespoons olive oil

- 3 cloves garlic, minced
- ¼ cup dry white wine (optional)
- 2 tablespoons lemon juice
- 2 tablespoons butter
- ¼ cup chopped fresh parsley
- Salt and freshly ground black pepper to taste
- 2 medium zucchini, spiralized or thinly sliced

Instructions:

- Heat olive oil in a large skillet over medium heat. Add garlic and cook until fragrant, about 30 seconds.
- Add shrimp and cook until pink and opaque, about 3-4 minutes per side.
- If using, add white wine and cook for 1 minute, allowing alcohol to evaporate.
- Stir in lemon juice, butter, and parsley. Season with salt and pepper to taste.
- Toss zucchini noodles with shrimp scampi sauce and serve immediately.

Serving Suggestion: Garnish with grated Parmesan cheese (if tolerated).

25. Beef Stir-Fry with Brown Rice

Ingredients:

- 1 pound lean beef sirloin, thinly sliced
- 2 tablespoons olive oil
- 1 onion, sliced
- 2 cloves garlic, minced
- 1 red bell pepper, sliced
- 1 green bell pepper, sliced
- 1 cup broccoli florets
- ½ cup snow peas
- ½ cup low-sodium soy sauce or tamari
- 2 tablespoons honey
- 1 tablespoon cornstarch
- 1 cup brown rice, cooked according to package directions

Instructions:

- In a small bowl, whisk together soy sauce, honey, and cornstarch. Set aside.

- Heat 1 tablespoon olive oil in a large skillet or wok over medium-high heat. Add beef and cook until browned, about 2-3 minutes per side. Remove beef from skillet and set aside.
- Add remaining olive oil to the skillet. Add onion, garlic, and bell peppers. Cook until vegetables are tender-crisp, about 5-7 minutes.
- Add broccoli and snow peas. Cook for 2-3 minutes more.
- Return beef to the skillet. Pour soy sauce mixture over beef and vegetables. Cook until sauce thickens, about 1-2 minutes.
- Serve stir-fry over brown rice.

Serving Suggestion: Garnish with chopped green onions or sesame seeds.

26. Chicken and Vegetable Skewers

Ingredients:

- 1 pound boneless, skinless chicken breasts, cut into 1-inch cubes
- 1 red bell pepper, cut into 1-inch pieces
- 1 green bell pepper, cut into 1-inch pieces
- 1 onion, cut into 1-inch pieces
- 1 zucchini, cut into 1-inch pieces
- 12 cherry tomatoes
- ¼ cup olive oil
- 2 tablespoons lemon juice
- 1 teaspoon dried oregano
- ½ teaspoon garlic powder
- Salt and freshly ground black pepper to taste

Instructions:

- In a large bowl, combine chicken, bell peppers, onion, zucchini, and cherry tomatoes.

- In a small bowl, whisk together olive oil, lemon juice, oregano, garlic powder, salt, and pepper. Pour over chicken and vegetables. Toss to coat.
- Thread chicken and vegetables onto skewers.
- Grill skewers over medium heat for 10-12 minutes, or until chicken is cooked through and vegetables are tender. Alternatively, bake skewers in a preheated oven at 400°F (200°C) for 15-20 minutes.

Serving Suggestion: Serve with a side of brown rice or quinoa salad.

27. Pork Tenderloin with Roasted Root Vegetables

Ingredients:

- 1 (1-pound) pork tenderloin
- 1 tablespoon olive oil
- 1 teaspoon dried rosemary
- ½ teaspoon garlic powder

- Salt and freshly ground black pepper to taste
- 1 pound root vegetables (such as carrots, parsnips, and sweet potatoes), peeled and cut into 1-inch pieces

Instructions:

- Preheat oven to 400°F (200°C). Line a baking sheet with parchment paper.
- Rub pork tenderloin with olive oil, rosemary, garlic powder, salt, and pepper.
- Place pork tenderloin on the prepared baking sheet. Arrange root vegetables around the pork.
- Roast for 20-25 minutes, or until pork is cooked through and vegetables are tender.

Serving Suggestion: Serve with a side of steamed green beans or a mixed green salad.

28. Baked Cod with Lemon and Herbs

Ingredients:

- 4 (4-ounce) cod fillets
- 1 tablespoon olive oil
- 1 lemon, thinly sliced
- 2 sprigs fresh thyme
- 2 sprigs fresh parsley
- Salt and freshly ground black pepper to taste

Instructions:

- Preheat oven to 400°F (200°C). Line a baking sheet with parchment paper.
- Place cod fillets on the prepared baking sheet. Drizzle with olive oil and top with lemon slices, thyme, and parsley.
- Season with salt and pepper to taste.
- Bake for 12-15 minutes, or until cod is cooked through and flakes easily with a fork.

Serving Suggestion: Serve with a side of roasted asparagus or steamed broccoli.

29. Ground Turkey Chili

Ingredients:

- 1 tablespoon olive oil
- 1 onion, chopped
- 2 cloves garlic, minced
- 1 pound ground turkey
- 1 (15-ounce) can diced tomatoes, undrained
- 1 (15-ounce) can kidney beans, rinsed and drained (optional, check with your dietitian)
- 1 (15-ounce) can black beans, rinsed and drained
- 1 cup vegetable broth (low-sodium)
- 1 tablespoon chili powder
- 1 teaspoon cumin
- ½ teaspoon oregano
- Salt and freshly ground black pepper to taste

Instructions:

- Heat olive oil in a large pot over medium heat. Add onion and garlic and cook until softened, about 5 minutes.
- Add ground turkey and cook until browned, breaking it up with a spoon.
- Stir in diced tomatoes, kidney beans (if using), black beans, vegetable broth, chili powder, cumin, oregano, salt, and pepper.
- Bring to a boil, then reduce heat and simmer for 30 minutes, or until flavors have melded.

Serving Suggestion: Top with chopped cilantro, avocado, or a dollop of plain Greek yogurt (if tolerated).

30. Vegetarian Lasagna

Ingredients:

- 9 lasagna noodles (oven-ready or no-boil)
- 1 tablespoon olive oil
- 1 onion, chopped

- 2 cloves garlic, minced
- 1 (28-ounce) can crushed tomatoes
- 1 (15-ounce) can tomato sauce (low-sodium)
- 1 teaspoon dried oregano
- ½ teaspoon dried basil
- Salt and freshly ground black pepper to taste
- 1 (15-ounce) container ricotta cheese (part-skim)
- 1 cup shredded mozzarella cheese (part-skim)
- ½ cup grated Parmesan cheese (optional, check with your dietitian)
- 1 cup frozen spinach, thawed and squeezed dry
- 1 cup sliced mushrooms

Instructions:

- Preheat oven to 375°F (190°C).

- Heat olive oil in a large skillet over medium heat. Add onion, garlic, and mushrooms. Cook until softened, about 5 minutes.
- Stir in crushed tomatoes, tomato sauce, oregano, basil, salt, and pepper. Bring to a simmer and cook for 15 minutes.
- In a medium bowl, combine ricotta cheese, mozzarella cheese, Parmesan cheese (if using), and spinach.
- In a 9x13 inch baking dish, spread a thin layer of tomato sauce. Top with a layer of lasagna noodles, followed by half of the ricotta cheese mixture. Repeat layers. Top with remaining tomato sauce and sprinkle with mozzarella cheese.
- Bake for 30-35 minutes, or until cheese is melted and bubbly. Let stand for 10 minutes before serving.

Serving Suggestion: Serve with a side salad.

Remember these key points for a kidney-friendly diet:

Limit sodium: Use low-sodium or no-salt-added ingredients and seasonings.

Control potassium: Be mindful of high-potassium foods and adjust portion sizes accordingly.

Manage phosphorus: Limit high-phosphorus foods like dairy products and processed foods.

Enjoy creating these delicious and nutritious meals!

Chapter 4: Side Dishes

31. Roasted Brussels Sprouts with Balsamic Glaze

Ingredients:

- 1 pound Brussels sprouts, trimmed and halved
- 2 tablespoons olive oil
- 1 tablespoon balsamic vinegar
- 1 teaspoon garlic powder
- ½ teaspoon dried thyme
- Salt and pepper to taste (use sparingly)

Instructions:

- Preheat oven to 400°F (200°C).
- In a large bowl, toss Brussels sprouts with olive oil, balsamic vinegar, garlic powder, and thyme.
- Spread Brussels sprouts in a single layer on a baking sheet.

- Roast for 20-25 minutes, or until tender and slightly browned.
- Season with salt and pepper to taste (remember to use salt sparingly).

Serving Suggestion: Serve as a side dish with grilled chicken or fish.

32. Steamed Green Beans with Lemon

Ingredients:

- 1 pound fresh green beans, trimmed
- 1 tablespoon olive oil
- 1 tablespoon lemon juice
- ½ teaspoon garlic powder
- Salt and pepper to taste (use sparingly)

Instructions:

- Steam green beans until tender-crisp, about 5-7 minutes.
- In a small bowl, whisk together olive oil, lemon juice, and garlic powder.

- Toss steamed green beans with the lemon dressing.
- Season with salt and pepper to taste (use sparingly).

Serving Suggestion: Serve as a light and refreshing side dish with any meal.

33. Mashed Cauliflower

Ingredients:

- 1 head cauliflower, cut into florets
- 2 tablespoons low-sodium broth or milk
- 1 tablespoon olive oil
- 1 teaspoon garlic powder
- Salt and pepper to taste (use sparingly)

Instructions:

- Steam or boil cauliflower until very tender, about 10-15 minutes.
- Drain cauliflower well and transfer to a food processor or blender.
- Add broth or milk, olive oil, and garlic powder.

- Process until smooth and creamy.
- Season with salt and pepper to taste (use sparingly).

Serving Suggestion: A healthy alternative to mashed potatoes.

34. Roasted Sweet Potatoes

Ingredients:

- 2 medium sweet potatoes, peeled and cubed
- 2 tablespoons olive oil
- ½ teaspoon cinnamon
- ¼ teaspoon nutmeg
- Salt and pepper to taste (use sparingly)

Instructions:

- Preheat oven to 400°F (200°C).
- In a large bowl, toss sweet potatoes with olive oil, cinnamon, and nutmeg.
- Spread sweet potatoes in a single layer on a baking sheet.

- Roast for 20-25 minutes, or until tender and slightly browned.
- Season with salt and pepper to taste (use sparingly).

Serving Suggestion: A naturally sweet and satisfying side dish.

35. Quinoa Pilaf

Ingredients:

- 1 cup quinoa, rinsed
- 2 cups low-sodium broth
- 1 tablespoon olive oil
- ½ cup chopped onion
- ½ cup chopped carrots
- ½ cup chopped celery
- Salt and pepper to taste (use sparingly)

Instructions:

- Heat olive oil in a saucepan over medium heat.
- Add onion, carrots, and celery and cook until softened, about 5 minutes.

- Add quinoa and broth. Bring to a boil, then reduce heat and simmer for 15-20 minutes, or until quinoa is cooked through and liquid is absorbed.
- Fluff with a fork and season with salt and pepper to taste (use sparingly).

Serving Suggestion: A versatile side dish that pairs well with chicken, fish, or vegetarian dishes.

36. Brown Rice with Herbs

Ingredients:

- 1 cup brown rice, rinsed
- 2 cups low-sodium broth
- 1 tablespoon olive oil
- 1 teaspoon dried herbs (such as thyme, rosemary, or oregano)
- Salt and pepper to taste (use sparingly)

Instructions:

- Combine rice, broth, olive oil, and herbs in a saucepan.

- Bring to a boil, then reduce heat and simmer for 45-50 minutes, or until rice is tender and liquid is absorbed.
- Fluff with a fork and season with salt and pepper to taste (use sparingly).

Serving Suggestion: A hearty and flavorful side dish.

37. Steamed Broccoli with Garlic

Ingredients:

- 1 head broccoli, cut into florets
- 1 tablespoon olive oil
- 2 cloves garlic, minced
- Salt and pepper to taste (use sparingly)

Instructions:

- Steam broccoli until tender-crisp, about 5-7 minutes.
- In a small pan, heat olive oil over low heat. Add garlic and cook until fragrant, about 1 minute.
- Toss steamed broccoli with garlic oil.

- Season with salt and pepper to taste (use sparingly).

Serving Suggestion: A simple and nutritious side dish.

38. Roasted Carrots and Parsnips

Ingredients:

- 1 pound carrots, peeled and sliced
- 1 pound parsnips, peeled and sliced
- 2 tablespoons olive oil
- 1 teaspoon dried thyme
- Salt and pepper to taste (use sparingly)

Instructions:

- Preheat oven to 400°F (200°C).
- In a large bowl, toss carrots and parsnips with olive oil and thyme.
- Spread vegetables in a single layer on a baking sheet.
- Roast for 20-25 minutes, or until tender and slightly browned.

- Season with salt and pepper to taste (use sparingly).

Serving Suggestion: A colorful and flavorful side dish.

39. Baked Acorn Squash

Ingredients:

- 1 acorn squash, halved and seeded
- 1 tablespoon olive oil
- 1 tablespoon maple syrup (optional)
- Salt and pepper to taste (use sparingly)

Instructions:

- Preheat oven to 375°F (190°C).
- Place squash halves cut-side up on a baking sheet.
- Drizzle with olive oil and maple syrup (if using).
- Bake for 45-60 minutes, or until tender.
- Season with salt and pepper to taste (use sparingly).

Serving Suggestion: A delicious and satisfying side dish.

40. Green Salad with Vinaigrette Dressing

Ingredients:

- 4 cups mixed greens
- ½ cup chopped cucumber
- ½ cup chopped tomatoes
- ¼ cup chopped red onion
- Vinaigrette dressing (see recipe below)

Instructions:

- Combine greens, cucumber, tomatoes, and onion in a large bowl.
- Toss with vinaigrette dressing.

Vinaigrette Dressing:

- 2 tablespoons olive oil
- 1 tablespoon balsamic vinegar
- 1 teaspoon Dijon mustard

Salt and pepper to taste (use sparingly)

Instructions:

- Whisk together all ingredients in a small bowl.

Serving Suggestion: A refreshing and versatile salad.

Important Notes for Kidney-Friendly Cooking:

Sodium: Use salt substitutes or herbs and spices to flavor your dishes instead of salt.

Potassium: Limit high-potassium ingredients like potatoes, tomatoes, and bananas.

Phosphorus: Be mindful of phosphorus content, especially in dairy products and processed foods.

Fluid: Monitor your fluid intake as directed by your doctor.

Remember to always consult with your doctor or a registered dietitian for personalized dietary advice.

Chapter 5: Snacks & Sweet Treats

These snacks are designed to be kidney-friendly, but always check with your dietitian or doctor for personalized advice as individual needs may vary.

41. Apple Slices with Almond Butter

Ingredients:

- 1 medium apple (such as Gala, Fuji, or Honeycrisp)
- 2 tablespoons almond butter (no salt added)

Instructions:

- Wash and core the apple.
- Slice the apple into thin wedges.
- Spread each apple slice with almond butter.

Serving Suggestion: Enjoy as a quick and easy snack. Pair with a small handful of almonds for extra protein and healthy fats.

42. Rice Cakes with Hummus and Cucumber

Ingredients:

- 2 brown rice cakes
- 2 tablespoons hummus (low-sodium)
- 1/4 cucumber, thinly sliced

Instructions:

- Spread each rice cake with hummus.
- Top with cucumber slices.

Serving Suggestion: This makes a light and refreshing snack. For added flavor, sprinkle with paprika or a pinch of red pepper flakes.

43. Fruit Salad with Low-Fat Yogurt

Ingredients:

- 1 cup mixed fresh fruit (such as berries, grapes, melon, and pineapple)
- 1/2 cup low-fat plain yogurt

Instructions:

- Wash and prepare the fruit (cut into bite-sized pieces as needed).
- Combine the fruit in a bowl.
- Top with low-fat yogurt.

Serving Suggestion: This is a refreshing and vitamin-packed snack. You can add a drizzle of honey or a sprinkle of chopped nuts for extra flavor and texture.

44. Hard-Boiled Eggs

Ingredients:

- 2 eggs

Instructions:

- Place eggs in a saucepan and cover with cold water.
- Bring the water to a boil over medium-high heat.
- Once boiling, reduce heat to low, cover the pan, and simmer for 8-10 minutes.
- Drain the hot water and immediately run cold water over the eggs until they are cool enough to handle.
- Peel the eggs and enjoy.

Serving Suggestion: Hard-boiled eggs are a great source of protein and can be enjoyed plain or with a sprinkle of black pepper.

45. Trail Mix with Nuts and Seeds

Ingredients:

- 1/4 cup unsalted almonds
- 1/4 cup unsalted walnuts or pecans
- 1/4 cup pumpkin seeds or sunflower seeds
- 1/4 cup dried cranberries or raisins (optional)

Instructions:

- Combine all ingredients in a bowl or reusable container.

Serving Suggestion: Enjoy a small handful as a satisfying snack. Be mindful of portion size, as nuts and seeds are high in phosphorus.

46. Greek Yogurt with Berries

Ingredients:

- 1 cup plain Greek yogurt (low-fat or non-fat)
- 1/2 cup mixed berries (such as blueberries, raspberries, and strawberries)
- Instructions:
- Top the Greek yogurt with berries.

Serving Suggestion: This is a protein-rich snack.

You can add a drizzle of honey or a sprinkle of granola for extra sweetness and crunch.

47. Angel Food Cake with Fruit

Ingredients:

- 1 slice angel food cake
- 1/2 cup sliced fresh fruit (such as strawberries, peaches, or kiwi)

Instructions:

- Top the angel food cake with fresh fruit.

Serving Suggestion: Angel food cake is low in fat and a good choice for a light dessert.

Enjoy with a dollop of low-fat whipped topping if desired.

48. Fruit Popsicles

Ingredients:

- 1 cup mixed fruit (such as berries, mango, or pineapple)
- 1/2 cup water or 100% fruit juice (low-potassium options like apple or cranberry juice)

Instructions:

- Blend fruit and liquid until smooth.
- Pour the mixture into popsicle molds.
- Freeze for at least 4 hours or until solid.

Serving Suggestion: A refreshing and hydrating treat, especially on warm days.

Choose fruits lower in potassium like berries, apples, and grapes.

49. Low-Sugar Oatmeal Cookies

Ingredients:

- 1 cup rolled oats
- 1/2 cup whole wheat flour
- 1/4 cup unsweetened applesauce
- 1/4 cup chopped walnuts or pecans (optional)
- 2 tablespoons maple syrup or honey
- 1 teaspoon cinnamon
- 1/2 teaspoon baking powder
- 1/4 teaspoon salt
- 1/4 cup water

Instructions:

- Preheat oven to 350°F (175°C).
- Combine dry ingredients (oats, flour, cinnamon, baking powder, and salt) in a large bowl.
- In a separate bowl, combine wet ingredients (applesauce, nuts, maple syrup/honey, and water).
- Add the wet ingredients to the dry ingredients and mix until just combined.
- Drop by rounded tablespoons onto a baking sheet lined with parchment paper.
- Bake for 12-15 minutes, or until golden brown.
- Let cool on a wire rack before serving.

Serving Suggestion: Enjoy these cookies in moderation as a healthier dessert option.

50. Dark Chocolate (small portion)

Ingredients:

- 1-2 squares (about 1 ounce) of dark chocolate (at least 70% cacao)

Instructions:

- Savor slowly and enjoy!

Serving Suggestion: Dark chocolate is rich in antioxidants and can be a satisfying treat.

Choose dark chocolate with minimal added sugar.

Important Notes:

Portion Control: Pay attention to portion sizes, especially for snacks higher in potassium, phosphorus, or sodium.

Fresh Ingredients: Whenever possible, use fresh fruits and vegetables.

Low-Sodium Options: Choose low-sodium or no-salt-added varieties of ingredients like nuts, nut butters, and hummus.

Read Labels: Always read food labels carefully to check for sodium, potassium, and phosphorus content.

Consult Your Dietitian: These recipes are suggestions, and it's essential to consult your dietitian or doctor for personalized dietary advice.

Chapter 6: Soups & Stews

51. Chicken Noodle Soup

Ingredients:

- 1 tablespoon olive oil
- 1 onion, chopped
- 2 carrots, chopped
- 2 celery stalks, chopped
- 8 cups low-sodium chicken broth
- 1 cup cooked chicken, shredded
- 1 cup whole wheat noodles
- 1/2 cup frozen peas
- 1/4 cup chopped fresh parsley
- Salt and pepper to taste (use sparingly)

Instructions:

- Heat olive oil in a large pot over medium heat. Add onion, carrots, and celery and cook until softened, about 5 minutes.
- Pour in chicken broth and bring to a boil. Add chicken and noodles. Reduce heat and

simmer for 10-15 minutes, or until noodles are cooked through.

- Stir in peas and parsley. Season with salt and pepper to taste.

Serving Suggestion: Serve hot with a side of whole-wheat bread.

52. Vegetable Beef Soup

Ingredients:

- 1 tablespoon olive oil
- 1 pound lean ground beef
- 1 onion, chopped
- 2 cloves garlic, minced
- 2 carrots, chopped
- 2 celery stalks, chopped
- 1 (14.5 ounce) can diced tomatoes, undrained
- 4 cups low-sodium beef broth
- 1 cup chopped potatoes
- 1 cup chopped green beans
- 1/2 cup frozen corn
- 1/4 cup chopped fresh parsley

- Salt and pepper to taste (use sparingly)

Instructions:

- Heat olive oil in a large pot over medium heat. Add ground beef and cook until browned, breaking it up with a spoon. Drain off any excess fat.
- Add onion and garlic to the pot and cook until softened, about 5 minutes.
- Stir in carrots, celery, tomatoes, beef broth, potatoes, and green beans. Bring to a boil, then reduce heat and simmer for 20–25 minutes, or until vegetables are tender.
- Add corn and parsley. Season with salt and pepper to taste.

Serving Suggestion: Serve hot with a dollop of low-fat sour cream or plain yogurt.

53. Tomato Basil Soup

Ingredients:

- 2 tablespoons olive oil
- 1 onion, chopped

- 2 cloves garlic, minced
- 2 (28 ounce) cans crushed tomatoes
- 4 cups low-sodium vegetable broth
- 1/4 cup chopped fresh basil
- 1 teaspoon dried oregano
- 1/2 teaspoon sugar
- Salt and pepper to taste (use sparingly)

Instructions:

- Heat olive oil in a large pot over medium heat. Add onion and garlic and cook until softened, about 5 minutes.
- Stir in crushed tomatoes, vegetable broth, basil, oregano, and sugar. Bring to a boil, then reduce heat and simmer for 15-20 minutes, or until flavors have melded.
- Season with salt and pepper to taste.

Serving Suggestion: Serve hot with a grilled cheese sandwich on whole-wheat bread.

54. Creamy Corn Chowder (low-sodium)

Ingredients:

- 1 tablespoon olive oil
- 1 onion, chopped
- 2 celery stalks, chopped
- 2 cloves garlic, minced
- 4 cups low-sodium chicken broth
- 2 (15.25 ounce) cans corn, drained
- 1 cup potatoes, diced
- 1/2 cup milk (or unsweetened almond milk)
- 1/4 cup cornstarch
- 1/4 cup water
- 1/4 cup chopped fresh parsley
- Salt and white pepper to taste (use sparingly)

Instructions:

- Heat olive oil in a large pot over medium heat. Add onion, celery, and garlic and cook until softened, about 5 minutes.

- Pour in chicken broth and bring to a boil. Add corn and potatoes. Reduce heat and simmer for 15-20 minutes, or until potatoes are tender.
- In a small bowl, whisk together milk and cornstarch until smooth. Slowly pour the cornstarch mixture into the soup, stirring constantly. Continue to cook until the soup has thickened.
- Stir in parsley. Season with salt and white pepper to taste.

Serving Suggestion: Serve hot with a side salad.

55. White Bean and Kale Soup
Ingredients:

- 1 tablespoon olive oil
- 1 onion, chopped
- 2 carrots, chopped
- 2 celery stalks, chopped
- 2 cloves garlic, minced
- 4 cups low-sodium vegetable broth

- 2 (15 ounce) cans cannellini beans, rinsed and drained
- 1 bunch kale, chopped
- 1 teaspoon dried oregano
- 1/2 teaspoon dried thyme
- Salt and pepper to taste (use sparingly)

Instructions:

- Heat olive oil in a large pot over medium heat. Add onion, carrots, celery, and garlic and cook until softened, about 5 minutes.
- Pour in vegetable broth and bring to a boil. Add cannellini beans, kale, oregano, and thyme. Reduce heat and simmer for 15-20 minutes, or until kale is tender.
- Season with salt and pepper to taste.

Serving Suggestion: Serve hot with a sprinkle of grated Parmesan cheese (if permitted in your diet).

56. Minestrone Soup

Ingredients:

- 1 tablespoon olive oil
- 1 onion, chopped
- 2 carrots, chopped
- 2 celery stalks, chopped
- 2 cloves garlic, minced
- 4 cups low-sodium vegetable broth
- 1 (14.5 ounce) can diced tomatoes, undrained
- 1 cup chopped zucchini
- 1 cup chopped green beans
- 1/2 cup chopped cabbage
- 1/4 cup small pasta (like ditalini or macaroni)
- 1/4 cup chopped fresh parsley
- 1/4 cup grated Parmesan cheese (optional, if permitted in your diet)
- Salt and pepper to taste (use sparingly)

Instructions:

- Heat olive oil in a large pot over medium heat. Add onion, carrots, celery, and garlic and cook until softened, about 5 minutes.
- Stir in vegetable broth, tomatoes, zucchini, green beans, and cabbage. Bring to a boil, then reduce heat and simmer for 15 minutes.
- Add pasta and cook until tender, about 8-10 minutes.
- Stir in parsley and Parmesan cheese (if using). Season with salt and pepper to taste.

Serving Suggestion: Serve hot with a side of whole-wheat bread.

57. Chicken and Rice Soup

Ingredients:

- 1 tablespoon olive oil
- 1 onion, chopped
- 2 carrots, chopped
- 2 celery stalks, chopped
- 8 cups low-sodium chicken broth

- 1 cup cooked chicken, shredded
- 1/2 cup uncooked long-grain rice
- 1/4 cup chopped fresh parsley
- Salt and pepper to taste (use sparingly)

Instructions:

- Heat olive oil in a large pot over medium heat. Add onion, carrots, and celery and cook until softened, about 5 minutes.
- Pour in chicken broth and bring to a boil. Add chicken and rice. Reduce heat and simmer for 15-20 minutes, or until rice is cooked through.
- Stir in parsley. Season with salt and pepper to taste.

Serving Suggestion: Serve hot with a side of steamed vegetables.

58. Beef Stew with Root Vegetables

Ingredients:

- 1 tablespoon olive oil
- 1 pound beef stew meat, cut into 1-inch cubes
- 1 onion, chopped
- 2 cloves garlic, minced
- 4 cups low-sodium beef broth
- 1 cup potatoes, diced
- 1 cup carrots, chopped
- 1 cup parsnips, chopped
- 1/2 cup turnips, diced
- 1 teaspoon dried thyme
- 1/2 teaspoon dried rosemary
- Salt and pepper to taste (use sparingly)

Instructions:

- Heat olive oil in a large pot or Dutch oven over medium-high heat.

- Add beef cubes and cook until browned on all sides.
- Add onion and garlic to the pot and cook until softened, about 5 minutes.
- Pour in beef broth, potatoes, carrots, parsnips, turnips, thyme, and rosemary. Bring to a boil, then reduce heat, cover, and simmer for 1 1/2 - 2 hours, or until beef and vegetables are tender.
- Season with salt and pepper to taste.

Serving Suggestion: Serve hot with a side of whole-wheat bread or biscuits (if permitted in your diet).

59. Lentil Stew with Spinach

Ingredients:

- 1 tablespoon olive oil
- 1 onion, chopped
- 2 carrots, chopped
- 2 celery stalks, chopped
- 2 cloves garlic, minced
- 4 cups low-sodium vegetable broth

- 1 cup brown or green lentils, rinsed
- 1 (14.5 ounce) can diced tomatoes, undrained
- 1 teaspoon dried cumin
- 1/2 teaspoon dried coriander
- 5 ounces baby spinach, chopped
- Salt and pepper to taste (use sparingly)

Instructions:

- Heat olive oil in a large pot over medium heat. Add onion, carrots, celery, and garlic and cook until softened, about 5 minutes.
- Pour in vegetable broth, lentils, tomatoes, cumin, and coriander. Bring to a boil, then reduce heat, cover, and simmer for 30-40 minutes, or until lentils are tender.
- Stir in spinach and cook until wilted, about 2 minutes.
- Season with salt and pepper to taste.

Serving Suggestion: Serve hot with a dollop of plain yogurt or a sprinkle of chopped fresh cilantro.

60. Turkey Chili with Beans

Ingredients:

- 1 tablespoon olive oil
- 1 onion, chopped
- 2 cloves garlic, minced
- 1 pound ground turkey
- 1 (15 ounce) can black beans, rinsed and drained
- 1 (15 ounce) can kidney beans, rinsed and drained
- 1 (14.5 ounce) can diced tomatoes, undrained
- 2 cups low-sodium chicken broth
- 1 tablespoon chili powder
- 1 teaspoon cumin
- 1/2 teaspoon oregano
- Salt and pepper to taste (use sparingly)

Instructions:

- Heat olive oil in a large pot over medium heat. Add onion and garlic and cook until softened, about 5 minutes.

- Add ground turkey and cook until browned, breaking it up with a spoon. Drain off any excess fat.
- Stir in black beans, kidney beans, tomatoes, chicken broth, chili powder, cumin, and oregano. Bring to a boil, then reduce heat, cover, and simmer for 30 minutes, or until flavors have melded.
- Season with salt and pepper to taste.

Serving Suggestion: Serve hot with a dollop of low-fat sour cream or plain yogurt, and a sprinkle of chopped fresh cilantro.

Important Notes for All Recipes:

Sodium: Use low-sodium or no-salt-added broths and canned goods whenever possible. Be mindful of added salt and use it sparingly.

Potassium: Some vegetables can be higher in potassium. If you have restrictions, consider leaching potatoes and other root vegetables before adding them to soups and stews. (To leach, soak chopped vegetables in water for a few hours, then drain and rinse.)

Phosphorus: Limit the use of dairy products, as they can be high in phosphorus. Consider alternatives like unsweetened almond milk or rice milk.

Fluids: Soups and stews contribute to your fluid intake. If you have fluid restrictions, be sure to factor this into your daily allowance.

Individual Needs: Always consult with your doctor or registered dietitian to ensure these recipes align with your specific dietary restrictions and health needs.

Substitutions: Feel free to experiment with different vegetables, beans, and protein sources to create your own variations.

Conclusion

• Living Well with a Kidney Transplant

A kidney transplant is a remarkable gift, a chance to reclaim your health and embrace life with renewed vigor.

But it's also a significant adjustment, requiring a lifelong commitment to self-care. Living well with a kidney transplant involves a holistic approach that encompasses physical health, emotional well-being, and a mindful approach to daily life.

"The Kidney Transplant Diet Cookbook" is your partner on this journey, providing guidance and support as you navigate this new chapter.

Nourishing Your Body:

Your new kidney, along with the medications you'll be taking, require careful attention to your diet. This means:

Prioritizing nutrient-rich foods: Focus on a balanced diet filled with fruits, vegetables, whole grains, and lean protein sources.

Managing fluid and electrolyte balance: Pay close attention to your fluid intake and be mindful of sodium, potassium, and phosphorus levels in your food.

Maintaining a healthy weight: Strive to achieve and maintain a healthy weight to reduce stress on your new kidney and lower your risk of complications.

Beyond the Plate:

Living well extends beyond your dietary choices. It's about nurturing your overall well-being:

Staying active: Regular physical activity is crucial for maintaining a healthy weight, improving cardiovascular health, and boosting your mood.

Managing stress: Practice stress-reduction techniques like meditation, deep breathing, or yoga to promote emotional well-being and support your immune system.

Prioritizing sleep: Aim for 7-8 hours of quality sleep each night to allow your body to repair and rejuvenate.

Building a support system: Connect with fellow transplant recipients, family, and friends to share experiences, gain support, and foster a sense of community.

Regular medical checkups: Attend all scheduled medical appointments and follow your healthcare provider's recommendations for ongoing monitoring and care.

Embracing a kidney transplant is an opportunity to redefine your relationship with your body and prioritize your health.

By adopting a holistic approach that combines mindful eating, regular exercise, stress management, and a strong support system, you can thrive in this new chapter and live a fulfilling life.

• Resources and Support

Your journey after a kidney transplant extends beyond the kitchen.

It's a path often shared with a network of healthcare professionals, support groups, and fellow transplant recipients.

These resources offer a wealth of knowledge, encouragement, and understanding that can significantly enhance your post-transplant life.

This book, while a valuable tool, is just one piece of the puzzle.

Connect with your transplant team, including your nephrologist, transplant coordinator, and dietitian. They are your primary sources of personalized guidance and medical expertise.

Consider joining a support group, either in person or online. Sharing experiences with others who understand your challenges and triumphs can provide invaluable emotional support and practical advice.

These connections foster a sense of community and remind you that you're not alone.

Remember, organizations dedicated to kidney health and transplantation offer a wealth of information and resources.

Explore their websites, attend their events, and tap into their expertise.

Finally, don't underestimate the power of your personal support network.

Lean on your family and friends for encouragement, understanding, and assistance as you navigate this new chapter.

By embracing these resources and building a strong support system, you'll be well-equipped to thrive after your kidney transplant.

This journey is a testament to your resilience, and you don't have to walk it alone.

Made in the USA
Las Vegas, NV
31 March 2025

20327369R00066